# HIS PEACE

### SEVEN DAYS OF PEACE ACTIVATION AND JOURNAL

## NYESHA GREER

Dedication

I dedicate this book to my God, who is the Great Lord God Jehovah. Thank you for showing me your power at work in my life. Thank you for allowing me to scribe your heart for the people of God. I am filled with great love and adoration for you Lord that will never go away.

-Your daughter, Nyesha

# Contents

| | |
|---|---|
| Introduction | 9 |
| At Peace with God | 11 |
| His Peace | 13 |
| His Prosperity | 15 |
| His Welfare, Well-being, and Healing | 19 |
| His Completeness and Wholeness | 23 |
| Command Your Peace | 27 |
| Peace Works with Faith | 31 |
| Staying in a Place of Peace | 35 |
| Living in Peace with Others | 37 |
| Practicing Peace | 41 |
| Conclusion | 45 |
| Seven Days of Peace. Activation and Journal | 47 |
| Confessions for God's Peace | 48 |
| Daily Confessions for Peace | 49 |
| Daily Prayers and Scripture Meditation | 50 |
| Additional Scriptures for Meditation | 91 |
| Final thoughts | 93 |
| Prayer of Salvation | 95 |

# Introduction

There is something you need to know about the peace of God. It is a gift to the body of Christ. In order to be called a true gift, it must be free of charge. We cannot work for it, and we cannot perform good deeds to possess such a gift. Our gift of peace has already been purchased with a price you and I will never be able to repay. Jesus fulfilled the payment for our peace. And right before leaving this earth, He made it a point to give His peace to us.

So, what is so special about His peace? It is full of power, and it covers every aspect of your life. It was strong enough to keep Christ focused on God's will though He encountered much opposition during His time of earthly ministry. His peace was strong enough to keep Him focused until He finished His Father's assignment at Calvary. This is what Jesus gave to you.

In this book, you will find how to live a life of peace, not only through the words written on this page, but as the Lord unveils His truth to your heart. You will begin to see areas where you have not experienced this peace. As this comes to you, begin to ask God to restore peace to you in those moments. And because of His great love for you, He will do what you have asked of Him.

As you read this book, I pray the Holy Spirit will begin to hover over you and bring revelation to your life so that by the end of this book, you are no longer the same. May your life be forever transformed into the life of peace God has always had in mind for you.

"Peace I leave with you; my peace I give you. I do not give to you as the world gives. Do not let your hearts be troubled and do not be afraid" (John 14:27, NIV).

*~Jesus*

# At Peace with God

Since the beginning of time, God has desired for us to walk with Him in fellowship and in peace. In Genesis, we see this desire manifested through a relationship He established with Adam, His very own creation. Adam was at peace with God and knew no sin. He was willfully living in submission to the Lord, and as a result, the Garden of Eden was the next best place to heaven. It was a paradise, fruitful and peaceful. When the serpent subtly enters the scene in Genesis 3, he craftily deceives Eve causing her to disobey God's command:

"16 And the Lord God commanded the man, saying, Of every tree of the garden thou mayest freely eat:

"17 But of the tree of the knowledge of good and evil, thou shalt not eat of it: for in the day that thou eatest thereof thou shalt surely die" (Genesis 2:16-17, KJV).

After being warned to not eat of the tree of the knowledge of good and evil, Adam and Eve disobeyed the command of the Lord, thus bringing sin into their lives. Peace with God had been removed, and sin, fear, and death enter their lives.

Sin is separation from God. When separated from Him, there is no peace with Him. Being at peace with God is not automatic because by nature you are separated from God. Romans 3:23 teaches us, "For all have sinned and fall short of the glory of God." Nonetheless, God had a plan to redeem mankind back into this place of peace and right standing with Him.

The scripture teaches us that there must be a payment for our sins, and Jesus paid the price in full all because of the great love the Father has towards us.

"For God so loved the world that He gave His only begotten Son, that whoever believes in Him should not perish but have everlasting life" (John 3:16).

God's love bridges the gap of separation between God and you. When Jesus Christ died on the cross and rose from the grave, the penalty for sin was paid in full.

"He personally carried the load of our sins in his own body when he died on the cross" (1 Peter 2:24, TLB). Amazingly, more was provided to us that day on the cross. More than just our sins were dealt with, but we also received back our right relationship with the Father, and that is where our peace flows from.

"But He was wounded for our transgressions, He was bruised for our iniquities; The chastisement for our peace was upon Him, and by His stripes we are healed" (Isaiah 53:5, NKJV). Jesus is our peace. Peace is not the absence of trouble; it includes everything that makes for man's greatest good.

The word peace used here is the Hebrew word shalom, meaning "peace, prosperity, wholeness, success, and well-being." He endured the punishment that made us completely whole. All of these have come to us through Christ's sufferings.

As a born-again believer, we have been made the righteousness of God in Christ Jesus. In return for Jesus taking our sin, those who put their faith in Him get His righteousness instead of their own. It's our trust in Jesus and what He has done that places His righteousness into our born-again spirits. Out of this place of right standing flows His beautiful Shalom—His Peace. Psalm 29:11 says, He "blesses His people with peace" (NIV). He did that through the blood of Jesus—the Prince of Peace (Isaiah 9:6).

# His Peace

Jesus said in John 14:26-27, "Peace I leave with you; My peace I give to you. I do not give to you as the world gives. Do not let your hearts be troubled; do not be afraid" (NIV). Jesus knew over 2,000 years ago we would need a peace that has the power to guard our hearts and minds while sojourning here on earth. He did not just leave us any ordinary peace that comes and goes with the trials and triumphs of life, but rather He gave the same peace that He himself utilized. So what is the mystery of His peace, and why was it just as essential to leave with us as the Spirit of God?

Webster's 1828 American Dictionary defines peace as a state of quiet or tranquility; freedom from disturbance or agitation; applicable to society, to individuals, or to the temper of the mind. It can refer to making peace, keeping the peace, holding the peace, or in a state of being at peace. However, according to the Hebrew root word for peace, or shalom, it bears more weight in meaning than that. Shalom refers to circumstances, one of well-being, tranquility, prosperity, and success. Shalom is a blessing. So in essence, Jesus pronounced a blessing over us, His people, in moments before His departure from earth. He left us with His well-being, His tranquility, His prosperity, and His wholeness without lack. Jesus handed over the greatest line of defense that we possess. Why is it the greatest? You and I have the power to keep this blessing in activation in our lives despite past, present, or future distractions or trouble. Our blessing of shalom cannot be removed, revoked, or denied. It truly belongs to us. Not only is peace, or shalom, a blessing, it is a promise given. This promise has been fulfilled through Jesus, our Savior. It is up to us to receive it.

So why are many of God's children not living in or experiencing this blessing of shalom? It's simple. We are either unaware that peace belongs to us in every way, or we have forfeited the right to possess it fully by way of trespass, transgression, or the deceitfulness of Satan. A trespass is a sin or wrongdoing. This sin could be against God or against someone else. When we allow sin to be in operation, we ultimately give way to the enemy's plans and schemes, and there is no peace in him. Transgressions are acts that go against a law, rule, or code of conduct. Biblically speaking, a transgression is the breaking of God's covenant. When this happens, we are no longer walking in peace, but on the contrary, we are opposing God. The deceitfulness of Satan is what I believe many believers are struggling with daily to overcome. This type of deceit comes subtly and more often than one would think. Whispers of defeat, hopelessness, lack, depression, and worthlessness appear on the screens of our minds to discourage us from believing we are complete in Christ in every facet of our lives. The scripture says in Ephesians 6:11, "Put on the whole armour of God, that ye may be able to stand against the wiles of the devil" (KJV). We have been given the armor of God so that when the attacks come, big or small, we can stand against the methods and strategies of the devil.

Right now is the time to build up your confidence and faith in what Jesus gave you—His peace. Peace has its own role to play in the life of a believer. Nevertheless, we must give it a place within us and allow it to work for us. Philippians 4:7 says, "And the peace of God, which transcends all understanding, will guard your hearts and your minds in Christ Jesus" (NIV) (emphasis mine). This word guard means to umpire. Just as an umpire calls a baseball game, that's the same implication that is being made here in the verse. God's peace will call or bring attention to those thoughts or situations that may arise that are designed to steal your peace. This blessing of peace works as a protective barrier against the turbulence of life. The scripture says this peace surpasses all understanding. In other words, it really may not make sense to you or the world, just how you are able to remain cool, calm, and peaceful when everyone else is losing their minds. This is why I believe Jesus gave His peace as a blessing because there is no way to maintain a place of tranquility in the natural. We must use His peace.

# His Prosperity

Prosperity is interconnected to the peace of God. Contrary to our modern understanding of prosperity, it does not simply refer to financial wealth, but it encompasses so much more. Prosperity denotes physical and spiritual goodness that only comes from God. The blessings we have in our lives can be traced back to the Lord's goodness towards us. God Himself is good. The scriptures are full of verses that give an account of His goodness throughout history. Psalm 86:5 declares, "You, Lord, are forgiving and good, abounding in love to all who call to you" (NIV).

David, in Psalms 23:6, is persuaded because the Lord is his Shepherd, goodness and mercy shall follow him all the days of his life. The essence of goodness is a derivative of God. Jesus teaches in Matthew 19:17 that there is only One who is good, and that is God, our Father. Goodness in the Old Testament typically signifies material blessings that were contingent upon the Israelites' ability to walk in obedience and remain free from sin. However, as a result of the finished work of Jesus Christ, we now benefit from God's goodness by receiving what Christ has already done for us.

Through our new covenant in Christ, we were given a free gift of peace and prosperity. Every gift God freely gives us is good and perfect, streaming down from the Father of lights, who shines from the heavens with no hidden shadow or darkness and is never subject to change (James 1:17 TPT). The Aramaic word used here for perfect, means "complete, wholesome, abundant, sufficient, enough, and perfect." Everything that God gives is complete. It is sufficient for us, it is perfect for us, and it is good for us. This is the God kind of prosperity. He desires for us as His children to walk in His peace that brings goodness into our daily lives. He has a plan to keep us in that peace if we are willing to keep our minds focused on Him. The writer in Isaiah 26:3 proclaims, "You will keep in perfect peace all who trust in you, all whose thoughts are fixed on you." (NLT) When we trust the Lord to do what He said He would do, we are free to place every burden and care upon on His shoulders. Jesus reminds us to cast all of our cares on Him because He deeply cares for us (1 Peter 5:7). It is comforting to know that our life's struggles, whether is it dealing with a hostile work environment or needing help to fall asleep at night, we know that if it is a care to us, it definitely qualifies as a care to Jesus.

God has chosen, based on His goodness, to keep us in peace, meaning this is a place we should dwell and not visit every once in a while. So let's evaluate where you are. Are you sitting on your couch thinking, I don't know when the last time I experienced peace was? It's been so long and life has just gotten so hard these past few years. I don't know where to begin. Often, we have spent more time focused on all that is going wrong, all of the disappointing situations in our life, all of the failures, and all of the pitfalls we've gone through instead of God's gleaming hope of goodness that He has given us.

Peace cannot be defined as a feeling or an emotional experience but rather a state of being in tranquility. God's goodness to you will lack nothing, and it is not easily troubled. Have you ever attempted to place something on a shelf, but when you let go of it to stand on its own, it falls over? You have repeatedly positioned it the way you desire on the shelf, but nothing you have done has helped. Then you say to yourself, I wish it would just stay put. At this point, you are frustrated and just about ready to forget the whole thing. Eventually you find a way to keep it on the shelf even if you have to give it some support to stand. Well, I dare say your peace has been that way. You attempted to position yourself in peace time and time again to no avail. And just like the object, you think, I wish I could just stay happy, stay in faith, and stay in peace. Perhaps, we should begin with our thinking. Dwelling on what we see in the natural actually works against what the scripture says.

Changing our mind has been the greatest challenge of our lives. If it were easy, we would all be living in a peaceful state, right? Romans 12:2 tells us, "Don't copy the behavior and customs of this world, but let God transform you into a new person by changing the way you think. Then you will learn to know God's will for you, which is good and pleasing and perfect" (NLT). Here, we are admonished to allow God to change our thinking. Generally, we attempt to do so on our own, but we truly need our Father's help. When He helps us, we are able then, and only then, to truly discern and know fully God's will for our lives, and His will is good, pleasing, and perfect. His Will is His plan to be good to us and through us. When we receive God's help, His goodness will resonate within our being, causing His prosperity to be seen in our lives by all we encounter as a result of operating in His peace.

# His Welfare, Well-being, and Healing

According to Dictionary.com, well-being can best be defined as the state of being healthy and happy; welfare, prosperity; the enjoyment of health and the common blessings of life. This flows from the peace of God into the lives of those who have been declared righteous by faith. Consider Romans 5:1, "Therefore, since we have been declared righteous by faith, we have peace with God through our Lord Jesus Christ" (CSB). By way of Christ, we have been made acceptable and placed in right standing with the Father. Our sins are no longer a barrier that stands in between us and God. When we repent before the Lord, He is quick to forgive us. This allows us to remain in a place of peace that was offered by Jesus and purchased on Calvary.

Isaiah 53:5 reveals Jesus as the one who carried the punishment for our peace. "But he was pierced for our transgressions, he was crushed for our iniquities; the punishment that brought us peace was on him, and by his wounds we are healed" (NIV). A great and horrible price was paid for us while we were yet in our sins through Jesus, our Savior. He willingly and obediently endured the cross and despised its shame for the joy that was set before Him (Hebrews 12:2). What possible joy could Christ have had in mind that would keep Him focused until finished while hanging on the cross, innocent, but yet carrying the sins of the world? His joy was you. His joy was in knowing you and I could become a son and daughter of God and live in His peace on earth and for eternity.

I would say our welfare and well-being was of utmost importance to God if He allowed His only son to suffer, so we could have peace between us and Him. Well-being not only refers to being in right standing with God, but it also shows His true desire for us to be in health. Let us examine the latter part of Isaiah 53: 5—"and by his wounds we are healed." This is a portion of scripture that is often quoted in relation to believing for healing from sickness and disease. At the same time, we now understand this verse openly displays the direct connection between peace and healing. According to this verse, this healing offered to believers does not mean partial healing or just feeling a little better. Instead, it implies nothing is missing, and nothing is broken—no illness, no sickness or disease. Jesus sealed the deal with His stripes so that we could fully enjoy the benefits and the blessings of the peace of God.

I believe the Lord is showing us through His word, His ultimate desire for His children is His Shalom, wholeness and health to our bodies. Like any contractual agreement, one must understand this agreement comes with benefits. So let me take a moment and explain what all can be healed through the works of Jesus. This healing is for any physical, emotional, or psychological issue you may be suffering from. I know the power of God is available to heal right now for those who believe. In addition to healing, He wants you to enjoy good health and the blessings of being alive in Christ. The evangelist John writes in 3 John 1:2, "Dear friend, I pray that you may enjoy good health and that all may go well with you, even as your soul is getting along well" (emphasis mine).

It is the will of God that we enjoy the life that Jesus came to give us in abundance. Sickness and sadness are not a part of His peace. As we begin to recognize what belongs to us through the peace that God gives, we should also perceive those things that do not belong to us and are not from God. This is where we allow peace to umpire within us. People typically do not need an umpire to call the obvious parts of a game. Instead, the most valuable, and sometimes game altering, moments happen when the umpire calls the "close calls." Those types of calls are often crucial and critical and are not always caught by everyone. So you see, it is not those obvious moments when Satan whispers in your ear to influence you to rob a store or lie on your time card at work, but rather it is the subtle suggestions that are made unbeknownst to you, such as Well, it's flu season, and I always get the flu. That statement cannot be found anywhere in scripture, especially concerning the new covenant through the blood of Christ. Those types of comments are well accepted in society, but they are absolutely from the pit of hell. The devil prides himself on the commonplace things we so easily agree to with little coercion from him. I can assure you that having the flu is undeniably a place of torment, not a place of peace. At the moment we finally realize that something is not from the Lord, our immediate response should be to reject those lies in the name of Jesus.

James 4:7 says, "Surrender to God! Resist the devil, and he will run from you" (CEV), We can resist by opposing what the devil is saying. His number one tactic is influence. If he can get us to believe his lies and deceit, we ourselves fall prey to his plan. However, the devil can be overcome, and God has given us the power and authority in Christ to do just that. If you are facing sickness, begin to read the word of God concerning healing. Say aloud, Healing belongs to me. I am in right standing with God through Christ. By the stripes of Jesus Christ, I AM healed!

As you do this, your mind will enter the transformation stage, and before you know it, your faith has increased and healing is manifesting itself in your mind, body, and soul. Remember, Jesus came to bring peace on earth, and without Him, there is no peace, completeness, healing, or wholeness.

# His Completeness and Wholeness

Christ offers us true completeness and wholeness through His peace. We find in Philippians 1:6, "being confident of this, that He who began a good work in you will carry it on to completion until the day of Christ Jesus." Paul is explaining to the church at Philippi that God has saved them and will bring their salvation to completion. When we accept Jesus as our Lord, He begins a good work in us—the work of salvation. In the very moment you accept Christ, you are born again. Born again simply means that you are now a new creature in Christ and the Holy Spirit of God lives in you. You have officially become a son or daughter of the Most High God. So what's new about you?

You have been made the rightful owner of a born-again spirit. That new spirit within you is 100% like God. The only trouble is that your mind does not fully know what to do.

God gave us His word to help transform our minds so that we can align our thinking with this new spirit we have inside. When the word of God gets in your heart and mind, it immediately sets out to repair brokenness and builds wholeness within you. The word can and will restore what is missing in your life. Brokenness comes from the enemy. It did not exist until Satan existed on earth. Understand that brokenness has affected all of us to some degree, but our Father can put the broken things back together. In our society, we reject what is broken. No one wants a broken phone, TV, or couch. We have those things repaired, and if they are beyond repair, we toss or exchange them for something new. Our God is not that way. The scripture says, "The Lord is close to the brokenhearted and saves those who are crushed in spirit" (Psalm 34:18 NIV). He is close to the brokenhearted and those He will not refuse. The Psalmist says in Psalm 51:17, "My sacrifice, O God, is a broken spirit; a broken and contrite heart you, God, will not despise." As a child of God, brokenness is an indication that we need to run towards Him, and He will put us back together again. Romans 8:28 is a promise that gives hope despite our broken lives. "And we know that in all things God works for the good of those who love Him, who have been called according to His purpose" (NIV).

Repairing the brokenness and restoring wholeness to you presents a lot of work to be done to your heart and mind, but this is where the Lord wants to work. He is excited about your transformation process and can't wait to for you to see the "you" He created you to be from the foundation of the world. Believe it or not, God sees the future you. The future "you" has a new walk, a new talk, and a heart that fully loves and believes God. It is easy to count ourselves out of this good work that has already begun in us because we continue to miss the mark and sin from time to time. Notice the scripture does not say that we are perfecting or bringing ourselves to completion. No, not at all. This is something God wants to do in us as we yield to His love and Holy Spirit, which has the power to change everything. You can have confidence now though you mess up and say the wrong thing, forget to pray, or not be very committed to reading His word, that God has started something good in you, and He is a finisher! He will see you through until the day of Christ Jesus. This may come as a little bit of a surprise, but your situations and circumstances do not shock God. He foreknew and still designed a destiny for you. Let me be clear. I am not saying that we have a license to sin and live recklessly knowing that God will work it all out later. By no means will that work. God's children love Him, and because we love Him, we obey Him fully, just as Christ did. We strive to give God our best each day He gives us the chance to do so. However, in the event we miss the mark, just know that God's grace has you covered.

Jeremiah 29 expresses the truth of how God foreknew what you would do for Him in the life you now have. He also knew that you and I would be a continual work in progress. But here lies a better promise. Philippians 1:6 tells us we can be confident, fully rely on, and trust with all of our heart, that the same God who started a good work in us, is Himself, bringing that work into completion. He is restoring what was lost, repairing the broken places of our hearts, and developing wholeness in us so that we can be complete and lacking nothing. The Lord has every intention to bring to maturity the work He has started. David writes in 138 Psalm, "The Lord will accomplish what concerns me." Wherever your weakness may be and whatever faults you may have, I pray you find comfort in knowing God is working in you.

# Command Your Peace

Late one evening after sending the multitudes away, Jesus and the disciples set out to cross over to the other side of the sea. While sailing across, a great storm arose. Wind beat against that boat while the waves poured in, threatening to sink it. The disciples were terrified and feared dying in the storm. But where was Jesus? He too was aboard the boat. What was His response to all of the commotion concerning the storm? Jesus was found by His disciples asleep on a pillow in the cabin below the deck. That's right! While everyone else was losing their minds in fear of death, Jesus was resting peacefully and completely unmoved by the menacing storm that was upon them. As people often do in response to a moment of fear, His disciples panicked and ran to wake Him saying, "Teacher, don't you even care that we are all about to drown" (Mark 4:38 TLB)?

What happens next is pretty intriguing and highly unexpected by all. Jesus does not run to the top of the boat and panic right along with them. He does not command all to jump ship in an effort to save them. What Jesus does next is exactly the first step to peace. Missing this step has continually prohibited God's people from walking in ultimate peace. This is a defining moment that distinguishes us from the world. Remember that Jesus gave us His peace right before His ascension to heaven. The disciples were His first witnesses to what peace was and what peace was truly created to do in the life of a believer. Jesus demonstrated a life lesson that is still applicable to us today.

The scripture says in Mark 4:39, "And he arose, and rebuked the wind, and said unto the sea, Peace, be still. And the wind ceased, and there was a great calm." There are a few critical components to note in this particular verse. Notice that He did not rebuke the disciples for a lack of faith, but rather He deals with what is causing the fear and chaos—the wind and sea. Why speak to the wind and sea first? The removal of fear and chaos is the presence of peace. Without dealing with the true issue behind their storm and fear, there could be no true peace. Here we see peace being used as a verb. It does something. What action took place that resulted in peace? Jesus spoke with His authority and commanded, "Peace, be still." The first step to peace is not to calm down but to remove chaos and fear that is being brought about by the devil.

Immediately the wind ceased, and there was a great calm. If you have ever stepped outside after a heavy storm has passed, you will see the sun show itself again. There is a peaceful stillness that sets in the atmosphere, and for a brief moment, all is calm in the world it seems.

I can only imagine that this must have been the feeling that was present after the storm ceased over them. Where did their fear go? Jesus removed the fear and the chaos of the wind, not only on the Sea of Galilee, but in the hearts of His disciples.

What can we gather from this demonstration of peace? First, we must understand peace does not come at random, and it is not automatic for the sons and daughters of God. We are equipped to use the authority we have been given through Christ and command those things in our lives that are bringing fear to cease. As it was with Jesus, so it is with us. We will soon find a great calm happening on the inside. Our peace flows from God. I feel it goes without saying that apart from God, you do not have peace. Many of us have looked for our peace in people, our careers, family, or material possessions, but quite frankly, we never truly tap into peace that way. While we can experience peace with those things in our lives, our peace simply does not come from them. Jesus says, "I give you my peace, not as the world gives." God's peace surpasses understanding because the world cannot define it.

The peace Jesus offers us is the same peace that was placed on display for us to see in Mark chapter four. The evil one will try to overwhelm you with the fears of this world just as he attempted that day on the Sea of Galilee. Fears and chaos swirl around us every day. Despite this ploy of

Satan, Jesus tells us to "be of good cheer, I have already overcome the world." He has overcome all fear, chaos, and disorder, and anxiety.

Blessed are the peacemakers for they shall be called the sons of God (Matthew 5:9 NIV). There is no higher relationship than to be a son. The peace of God flows from peace with God. Walking in His peace has everything to do with our relationship to the Father and our willingness to be obedient and trust in Him. With your relationship comes authority, and with authority comes the ability to command peace. Yes, your authority brings peace.

As a result, we can walk in peace with others through life circumstances as well as have peace all around us. You and I can be free of disturbance and enjoy a quiet demeanor despite the the condition of our city and our nation. We can live a life free of fear and full of calm and tranquility.

# Peace Works with Faith

Somehow there is a connection between our peace and our faith. We know according to Galatians 5:22-23, "But the fruit of the Spirit is love, joy, peace, long-suffering, gentleness, goodness, faith, meekness, temperance: against such there is no law." They both flow out of the same Spirit that God has given to you and me. As we walk by the Spirit of God, evidence should be seen in our lives of their existence.

Seemingly in the times we now live, peace is hard to find because we are constantly inundated with the cares of this fallen world. Having an understanding of how to operate in God's peace on a consistent basis is key to living the life Christ came to give in abundance. Note in John 10:10, Jesus clarifies His purpose for coming to the earth.

"The thief cometh not, but for to steal, and to kill, and to destroy: I am come that they might have life, and that they might have it more abundantly" (KJV).

The abundant life Jesus is referring to here in this verse is zóé (dzo-ay') life. This is life as God intended. Our Father planned for us to live in peace, not only with Him and with others, but in all things. While this is the Master's plan, peace will not come free of challenges, trouble, anxiety, or fear. In His infinite wisdom, He foreknew what situations and circumstances we would face in this life and knew we needed something that would possess the ability to cause us to stand and to remain in our rightful place as sons and daughters of God. He gave us His peace. This peace is a heavenly line of defense that allows us to circumvent the attacks of the enemy and live on earth in a place of faith.

If you are not experiencing this life that God has provided in abundance, then allow me to examine a possible reason why. Let us take another look at what Jesus said to His disciples after He calmed the storm in

Mark chapter four.

"And he said unto them, Why are ye so fearful? How is it that ye have no faith" (Mark 4:40, KJV)?

Jesus recognized the thief that had come to steal their peace. He called it by name—fear. Fear had crept into the hearts of the disciples, robbing them of their peace they once had. When fear came in, peace went out, leaving them with no hope.

Feeling hopeless is a clear sign that our peace is gone and fear has set in our hearts.

Fear is an offspring of Satan. It is designed to steal, kill, and destroy the blessings in your life. Faith and fear cannot cohabitate as they have different agendas and will produce two different outcomes in your life. Fear is not to be underestimated or to be taken lightly. It has been used as subtle as a thought to manipulate and deceive others as well as a form of power to take control of an entire nation of people. Fear can be a controlling force in your life, and its end is destruction. However, your faith is even more powerful than that. Jesus illustrates the power of believing in Mark 11:23.

"For verily I say unto you, That whosoever shall say unto this mountain, Be thou removed, and be thou cast into the sea; and shall not doubt in his heart, but shall believe that those things which he saith shall come to pass; he shall have whatsoever he saith" (KJV).

Jesus tells us we can speak to a mountain without having doubt in our hearts, and it will obey our command. Some might argue that this statement is just a figurative statement designed to explain the greatness of our faith. Even so, to move a mountain with only a faith-filled command is still an amazing ability the Lord has afforded to us. Our faith, not only in Jesus, but also in what we say, is a divine power given only by God Almighty.

For some of us, our peace has been removed because of others or life events that were beyond our control. No matter what the issue is, right now in this moment, God is offering your peace back to you. God's peace belongs to His children. He is giving you the wisdom and understanding to know that fear, anxiety, worry, and turmoil did not come from Him, and you do not have to receive those awful gifts from Satan.

The scripture says, "For God gave us a spirit not of fear but of power and love and self-control" (2 Timothy 1:17, ESV). So how do we live a life free from fear? If fear is interrupting your peace, you can take back your peace by your faith-filled words just as Jesus did. The operative phrase being "faith-filled." That's right. We must believe that peace, or shalom, has been given to us. You can rebuke and resist whatever the enemy is telling you and chose to believe what God says about you.

If this sounds too elementary to be powerful and effective, let me assure you the word of God works. I am not diminishing the reality of what you have been through or what you are facing now. As a fellow believer who works at keeping my own peace in tact from day to day, I know that we deal with all manner of evil. Some of you may have endured horrific seasons in your life. While we do not have the capacity to undo the damage in our lives or change the hurtful memories of times in the past, we can rejoice in knowing that our past is not our future. Only our God encapsulates the ability to take all of those pieces—the good, the bad, the ugly—and turn them into a beautiful masterpiece. Because you have breath in your body, you can become an awe-inspiring testament to the goodness and faithfulness of God. You are created in the image of God, and even now, your life has purpose. He wants you to live out your days in peace. My desire is for you to see everything that is coming against your peace is subject to change when you release the command for it to change in faith. Your peace can return the minute you deal with the fear, worry, anxiety, and turmoil coming against you.

Even if your problems do not change immediately, continue to stand in faith with your peace (Ephesians 6:14).

# Staying in a Place of Peace

We have been given the blessing of peace through our Lord Jesus Christ. At the very moment He stated to His disciples, "Peace I give you," we acquired everything that comes with the peace package. You must know by now, Satan does not want you to walk in this God-given peace. He wants you in turmoil, chaos, fear, and unbelief. But the truth is he himself has no power to control you. He utilizes influence by way of suggestive thought to prompt you to consider any other way than God's way. Not only do you have an enemy working against you, but there is also the weakness of the flesh. The scripture says in James 1:14, "Temptation comes from our own desires, which entice us and drag us away."

Our own lustful desires, also known as sin, pull us away from God's desire for us, which is to be in a place of shalom, His peace. Verse thirteen of this same chapter in the book of James clearly expounds on the character of God, the Father, "And remember, when you are being tempted, do not say, 'God is tempting me.' God is never tempted to do wrong, and he never tempts anyone else."

The Lord has no desire to do wrong nor to cause you to do what is wrong. He is a good Father to His children and has a plan to prosper each one of us. However, we do wrong sometimes—for some of us, on a regular basis. I believe we want to do what is right more often than not, but our flesh is weak. Unfortunately, we find ourselves in a trench of disgust and torment, disappointed that we can't seem to break the cycle. It is in this place that we are no longer walking in a place of peace but rather a place of defeat. So how can we change ourselves? I think many would agree that we would much rather keep our peace intact than to gratify the sinful desires of the flesh. While this is not an easy task to accomplish, thanks be unto God, there is hope for us. We know sin separates us from enjoying all that God has given to His children. It robs us of our peace and offers hopelessness in its place. But Christ is our hope. He is hope for a better tomorrow. He is hope that brings confidence in what God has promised. He is hope that reassures us that trouble will not last always.

The remarkable finished works of Jesus are still at work in our lives today. Jesus paid the price for our peace as well as our sin. Consider Isaiah 53:5, "He was wounded for our rebellious acts. He was crushed for our sins. He was punished so that we could have peace, and we received healing from his wounds" (GWT). The price that was paid for our peace could never be purchased by our own good works. We needed a Savior. We needed what only His sacrifice could provide. In the midst of sin, we can be forgiven and walk in peace. I've learned that God is not nearly as hung up over our sin as we have thought in the past. He knew we would need a perfect sacrifice to completely blot out our sin, so He sent the best thing heaven had to offer—His Son.

Our Father has made it so easy to return to Him. When you and I sincerely repent, turn from our ways of sin, and ask Him to forgive us, He is quick to forgive and forget them. Isaiah 43:25 says, "I—yes, I alone—will blot out your sins for my own sake and will never think of them again (NLT). The Great Lord God Jehovah choses to forget our sins. I am so thankful for this verse. We have a clean slate with God, and He made that decision before we ever needed His forgiveness. Why did He do that? Because He wants us to stay in a place of peace with Him always.

You must determine whether it is it the evil one working against you or is it you. If the devil is trying to hinder your life of peace, you have to make the decision to refuse his offer and trust what God says about your situation. Remember, the word of God is His Will for us. If the word says we can have it, then it belongs to us. Meditating on God's word is essential to overcoming any battle. Even though we have the victory through Christ, we must be resilient and continue to stand until we see what God has said concerning us. In order for the truth of God's word to be deeply planted within us and bear fruit, we have to keep it before us, read it, and mediate on it for as long as it takes to become truth to us. When this happens, you will stay in peace no matter what comes your way.

# Living in Peace with Others

"If possible, so far as it depends upon you, be at peace with all people" (Romans 12:18). This verse implies there is a responsibility for a believer to be at peace with all people. I'm sure you have thought of that one person who will make this task impossible. No matter who you are or where you live, we have all encountered individuals who can make it quite a challenge to be at peace with them. In fact, typically those people spur on the worst in you. So how can we be at peace with the difficult ones? Romans 12:18 begins by saying two key words, "If possible." Possible by definition means able, having power, powerful, or mighty. Only that which is in our power are we able to do. Anything above or beyond that measure, we are not responsible for. It is at this point that we must shake the dust from our feet and release them into the hands of God.

Please understand not everyone will receive us in peace. Not everyone will desire to live peacefully with others. We are not called to make them be at peace, but we are called to do the best we can to live peacefully with them. God has given us the blessing of His shalom, or His wholeness. Wherever we go, we must characterize His peace through our conduct towards others. We will not be judged based on how people treat us but rather how we treat them. I must admit it is trying to be a peace with someone who is rude and hateful towards you. However, if we can keep Christ in mind when we encounter such people, I believe our response to their behavior will be the greatest ministry to them and can potentially bring freedom from the bondage they are experiencing. People who are not peaceful towards others should not be classified as bad people. Something has happened to them either that specific day or prior to that day, and they need to encounter Jesus. His presence is so peaceful and can calm any tumultuous storm. You and I have the ability to bring Jesus into the room with us. Whether we are at the drive-thru window or standing in the checkout line at the local grocery store, Jesus is there. We carry Him within us. Being mindful of His glorious presence sets the tone for our mood and demeanor. We smile more when we know He is with us even when we come across a challenging person. In fact, I believe Jesus is looking for a way to minister to that individual that everyone hates to be around. He is looking for someone who is willing to not consider themselves and how they feel but rather consider the need of the one who is not at peace. We only observe the outside of those types of people but never truly see the torment that wreaks havoc in their hearts and minds every day. Even if they don't realize it, they are looking for the peace that only Jesus can give. The body of Christ is called to be carriers of this peace, or dispensers of hope to all that we meet. Unfortunately, we cannot spend our lives avoiding the difficult ones and befriending those that are most like us. At that rate, no one will ever change, and we are called to be world changers! We reach the world by going to them right where they are. Think about it. That's what God did for us. While we were yet sinners, Christ died (Romans 5:8, KJV). He did not wait for us to get our act together. He met us at our point of need.

Living in peace is a request from the Father's heart. As much as it depends on you and as much as is in your power, live in peace. There is only so much we can do, but if we are honest, we can do more. We can practice living in peace by watching what we say and how we say it. We can strive to live in peace by befriending the one person no one wants to be around. Even if they choose not to be friendly to us, we can, as often as the opportunity presents itself, smile, wave, be helpful, share, and compliment. When we display even the smallest act of kindness in our efforts to be at peace, we are releasing shalom in their lives, and Jesus is being made known in a very tangible way through us. In the last days upon earth, Jesus is taking every opportunity to win souls. Not so heaven can be heavily populated and there's more people in church on Sundays, but He is reaching for the ones His Father loves. For God so loved the world that He gave His only begotten Son, so that whosoever believes in Him should not perish but have everlasting life (John 3:16, KJV), God does not want to spend eternity without His creation. He is inviting us to participate in the drawing of His lost sheep.

Moreover, there are some believers who do not live in a place of peace for whatever the reason. As some circumstances would have it, they have been hurt, abused, or experienced traumatic events in their life, and it has left them bitter and without peace. Even though the body of Christ is the rightful heir to the peace of God, as long as they live in a place of bitterness, resentment, anger, or hate, they cannot enjoy the fullness of God's peace. The Lord wants them to live in it, but it is a choice to receive it from Him. So do we need to spend time on those believers who should know this already? Absolutely! Jesus' heart will not be hardened towards them. Even more so, He is drawn to them. Psalm 34:18 says, "The Lord is close to the brokenhearted and saves those who are crushed in spirit." The Lord wants to be near them because this is where they need Him the most. Living in peace is not just for us, but this peace is also a ministry to others—a ministry that Jesus Himself wants to be a part of right alongside of you. We may have to forgive some, so we can win them. Be prepared. You never know when the door will open for salvation or restoration. When it does, be found with the right heart, ready to be used by the Lord to bring them to Him. When you let your peace come upon them, you allow Jesus to be seen through you.

## Practicing Peace

One may find it challenging to live in a constant place of peace in the day and time we are in now. Everything seems unstable, and nothing remains the same. People can no longer rely on jobs, degrees, years of experience, spouses, income, or anything of the like. Burdensome times have a way of ciphering peace right out of your life. I think it goes without saying that this is not the will of God for His children. Nope, not at all. He gave us peace so that even in the face of arduous times, we could remain the same, unmoved by any outside factor. He designed us to be the ones to change our circumstances, not for our circumstances to change us. All the same, many of us have been affected. While we are in the world, we are not of the world, meaning whatever is rising against those that are in the world does not have the right to rise against us. We have been given an authority from Jesus to decree a thing, and it shall be established (Job 22:28, KJV). We can stay in a place of peace if we continue to practice this peace. Even as we strive to live in peace with others, so we bring peace into our own lives. Practicing peace is the remedy to those who need the return of peace in their life. It is as the law of sowing and reaping. What you sow is surely what you will reap. The peace you have sown may not necessarily be reaped from the person you are sowing it into, but it will return to you.

If you are not experiencing peace as you ought to, examine where the glitch might be. You might be surprised to find you may be at the root of the problem. Often, it is easy to be peaceful with co-workers or friends, but your spouse never receives that peace from you. They only see the contentious and belittling side of you. Our peace should begin in our home. Our children and spouses must receive peace from us so that Jesus can be demonstrated in their lives as well. When peace flows in your home, it sets the stage for many blessings to come upon you and your family. When those outside of our home enjoy being around us because we bring peace with us, but those we live with do not, it is a false witness of Christ that we share. When we practice peace, it should radiate in every arena we operate within. In the New Testament, the word eirene is used heavily in Paul's writings in 1 Corinthians 7. Here, the word peace could refer to the opposite of disorder. God expressly desires for spouses to live in a place of peace. Nothing much is accomplished within a marriage that is divided because of strife and disorder. Bring your peace to your spouse first, then to your children. Offer this peace to them as a love offering to the Lord. What do I mean by love offering? Show your love for the Lord through your willingness and obedience to walk in peace with those He has given to you. If your spouse is a non-believer but desires to remain married, continue to allow your peace to minister Jesus unto them (1 Corinthians 7:16). Your peace is a type of ministry within your own home. The unbelieving spouse may not listen to your sermons about going to church or getting saved, but they will receive your peace because it is full of the love of God. Through your peace, God will draw them. Practice this peace with all people. By practicing peace, we literally apply it to our daily lives in every way. Peace moves from the background of our faith as an idea, belief, or method and becomes the method of interacting with those around us. Peace cannot be another church cliché. God is calling for us to utilize what He has freely given us for our good and for the benefit of others. I think it is safe to say that when we increase walking in peace with others we increase our own level of experiencing peace. This may not be as easy as it sounds, especially when your relationships are on the verge of being destroyed or are so severely damaged you don't even know where to begin to repair the broken places. In order to restore peace, you need the help of the Lord. You need His wisdom and guidance on what to do and not do. That is right. Even your good intentions can have an adverse effect and be taken wrong, adding fuel to the fire. You need God to instruct you and lead you by His Holy Spirit in doing what is right. The scriptures say in Proverbs 14:12, "There is a way which seemeth right unto a man, but the end thereof are the ways of death" (KJV). You may have great intentions, but only God knows the heart of man. Not only will our

Father lead you into the most effective way of practicing peace, but He will also keep you in peace in the process. Sometimes when we offer our peace to others, they reject it. If we are not careful, this can bring us out of His peace and into dark places. God does not want us to be negatively affected. Out of His great goodness towards us, He has promised to keep us in perfect peace when our minds are stayed on Him. If we approach applying peace out of the wrong motives or wrong heart or for selfish reasons, we teeter along the lines of deception in the enemy's camp. It is out of a pure heart and a right spirit by which we will operate in His perfect peace.

If there are broken relationships in your life, whether it be with a parent, spouse, co-worker, or friend, it is time to seek the Lord and deal with the issues of our heart. Allow the Father to minister truth to you so you can be set free from any entanglement of the enemy. Then that peace you are truly seeking will begin to manifest in you and through you. At that moment, you can offer peace to others. It is only then you can practice real authentic peace in your daily life.

# Conclusion

God wants you to know that His peace is as real as He is. You cannot believe that He is a good Father and then spend the rest of your time on earth miserable. Take hold of this peace He has given you. Trust me, you won't need it in heaven. The need for peace is for now. Do not concern yourself with perfection. In the efforts of trying to perfectly execute walking in God's peace, you will miss God's peace. His peace has nothing to do with your ability to carry out any particular action. Through Christ, the work has been done for over 2,000 years. Our only part in this process is to receive what the Father has offered us through His son and allow Him to lead us the rest of the way. Even if God instructs us to do something, you can rest easy knowing that He intends to help you accomplish the smallest task if you let Him.

There is an urgency to understand His peace and your rights to it as a believer. The world will not take a turn for the better but rather grow worse as we see the final days approaching. This is not a place to worry or fret. We as believers should rejoice for our Savior will soon come. You will need to have the peace of God. Peace will not be found by the people in the world, but rather they will need to see His peace in your life. Practice this peace and use this peace wherever you go and with whomever you cross paths, for this could be a divine moment to be used by the Lord.

My prayer is that you have gathered a deeper revelation by the Holy Spirit of the true gift of God in your life, shalom. Use it, enjoy it, and give it away! The Father delights in seeing us enjoy His blessings, just as a parent will rejoice over the excitement of their own children when they bless them.

# Seven Days of Peace Activation and Journal

As you begin to meditate and pray concerning God's peace, or shalom, in your life, I pray you will experience the mighty presence of Jehovah Shalom in your life. For the next seven days, meditate, pray, and activate the blessing of His peace over yourself. Allow the Holy Spirit to lead you in this time of activation. He will reveal God's perfect peace to you in ways you have never known before. According to Matthew 11:24, use your faith to believe you receive when you pray, and you shall have it.

Christ died so that you could experience the shalom of God. You have this blessing of God right now in your life. It is time to activate the blessing of peace, so you can enjoy this wonderful portion of your inheritance.

To activate simply means to make something active or operative. It is not that you have been without God's shalom, but it is likely that it has not be in complete operation in your life. What good is a brand new car, fully paid for, sitting in your garage, if you never start and use it. Sure, peace is yours, but let's use it to enjoy better days. After all, that is the will of the Father.

Make daily confessions of peace, pray the prayers for peace, and meditate on the word of God concerning His peace, for His words are life to those who find it. Do not be limited by the suggested prayers but rather be led to pray by the spirit of God. I encourage you to write down whatever the Lord says or reveals to you in this time. Get ready to activate His glorious peace in your life.

# Confessions for God's Peace

I commit my life to peace and prosperity.

Jesus is my peace.

The Lord surrounds me in His peace.

I am blessed and prosperous because I choose to live in God's peace.

I will see good, do good to others, and will have many good days.

I am a peaceable person.

My life is good because I keep my tongue from evil.

I am quick to forgive, slow to speak, and slow to anger.

I am whole, prosperous, lacking no good thing.

All of my needs are met through God's riches and glory by Christ Jesus.

My mind and heart dwell in His shalom.

I receive the peace of God that passes all understanding.

The peace of God will guard my heart and my mind.

Jehovah will keep me in perfect peace.

Because the Lord has set His affection upon me, I will not fear.

Though I walk through valleys, I will fear no evil, for God is with me.

I refuse to be tormented by the devil, vexed, harassed, oppressed, poor or broke.

I have been redeemed from the curse of the law.

The Lord is my banner.

The Lord is my refuge.

I bring peace to others.

Peace is my atmosphere.

He is my Jehovah Shalom, my prosperity, and my peace.

He only is my rock and my salvation: He is my defense; I shall not be moved.

I will walk in peace all the days of my life.

# Day one

## Prayer

Father, thank you for your peace. Show me the way of peace. Allow your peace to rest in me and upon me. Allow me to share your peace with all those around me. Let your peace come to my house and find rest there. Let this peace be upon my children and all those connected to me and all that I have. Let peace be in my walls and prosperity within my palaces. Thank you, Lord, for your covenant of peace.

In Jesus' name. Amen.

## Confession

I commit my life to peace and prosperity.

Jesus is my peace.

The Lord surrounds me in His peace.

I am blessed and prosperous because I choose to live in God's peace.

# Scriptures for Meditation

**Romans 3:17 (NIV):** "and the way of peace they do not know."

AMPC: "And they have no experience of the way of peace [they know nothing about peace, for a peaceful way they do not even recognize]."

**Romans 15:33 (NIV):** "The God of peace be with you all. Amen."

AMPC: "May [our] peace-giving God be with you all! Amen (so be it)."

**1 Samuel 25:6 (NIV):** "Say to him: 'Long life to you! Good health to you and your household! And good health to all that is yours!"

AMPC: "And salute him thus: Peace be to you and to your house and to all that you have."

**Numbers 25:12 (NIV):** "Therefore tell him I am making my covenant of peace with him."

AMPC: "Therefore say, Behold, I give to Phinehas the priest My covenant of peace."

**Psalm 122:7 (NIV):** "May there be peace within your walls and security within your citadels."

AMPC: "May peace be within your walls and prosperity within your palaces!"

# Day one

# Day one

## Day one

# Day two

## Prayer

Thank you, Lord, that You give me strength and peace. Establish me in your peace today. Speak peace to me, God, and let me not turn back to folly. I will pursue those things that make peace. I pray that my ways will be pleasing to You so that You will make even my enemies to be at peace with me. Lord, let your peace guard my heart and mind this day. Keep my mind stayed on you, and I know that you will keep me in perfect peace. In Jesus' name. Amen.

## Confession

I am blessed and prosperous because I choose to live in God's peace.
I will see good, do good to others, and will have many good days.
I am a peaceable person.
My life is good because I keep my tongue from evil.

# Scriptures for Meditation

**Psalm 29:11 (NIV):** "The Lord gives strength to his people; the Lord blesses his people with peace."

AMPC: "The Lord will give [unyielding and impenetrable] strength to His people; the Lord will bless His people with peace."

**Isaiah 26:3 (NIV):** "You will keep in perfect peace those whose minds are steadfast, because they trust in you."

AMPC: "You will guard him and keep him in perfect and constant peace whose mind [both its inclination and its character] is stayed on You, because he commits himself to You, leans on You, and hopes confidently in You."

**Isaiah 26:12 (NIV):** "Lord, you establish peace for us; all that we have accomplished you have done for us.

AMPC: "Lord, You will ordain peace (God's favor and blessings, both temporal and spiritual) for us, for You have also wrought in us and for us all our works."

**Philippians 4:7 (NIV):** "And the peace of God, which transcends all understanding, will guard your hearts and your minds in Christ Jesus."

AMPC: "And God's peace [shall be yours, that tranquil state of a soul assured of its salvation through Christ, and so fearing nothing from God and being content with its earthly lot of whatever sort that is, that peace] which transcends all understanding shall garrison and mount guard over your hearts and minds in Christ Jesus."

**Proverbs 16:7 (NIV) :** "When the Lord takes pleasure in anyone's way, he causes their enemies to make peace with them."

AMPC: "When a man's ways please the Lord, He makes even his enemies to be at peace with him."

# Day two

## Day two

## Day two

# Day three

## Prayer

Father, thank you for your covenant of peace with me. It is an everlasting covenant that you will not break. Lord, you are not the author of confusion but of peace. I receive your clarity today in all that I set my hands to do. I will acquaint myself with You and be at peace, and good will come to me. I declare that I have the peace that you give me, not as the world gives; therefore, my heart will not be troubled. Allow me to be like the one who is blameless and upright so that my future will be that of peace. This day, I will be meek and delight myself in the abundance of your peace. In Jesus' name. Amen.

## Confession

I am quick to forgive, slow to speak, and slow to anger.

I am whole, prosperous, lacking no good thing.

All of my needs are met through God's riches and glory by Christ Jesus.

My mind and heart dwell in His shalom.

# Scriptures for Meditation

**Ezekiel 37:26 (NIV):** " I will make a covenant of peace with them; it will be an everlasting covenant. I will establish them and increase their numbers, and I will put my sanctuary among them forever."

AMPC: "I will make a covenant of peace with them; it shall be an everlasting covenant with them, and I will give blessings to them and multiply them and will set My sanctuary in the midst of them forevermore."

**1 Corinthians 14:33 (NIV):** "For God is not a God of disorder but of peace—as in all the congregations of the Lord's people."

AMPC: "For He [Who is the source of their prophesying] is not a God of confusion and disorder but of peace and order. As [is the practice] in all the churches of the saints (God's people),"

**John 14:27 (NIV):** "Peace I leave with you; my peace I give you. I do not give to you as the world gives. Do not let your hearts be troubled and do not be afraid."

AMPC: "Peace I leave with you; My [own] peace I now give and bequeath to you. Not as the world gives do I give to you. Do not let your hearts be troubled, neither let them be afraid. [Stop allowing yourselves to be agitated and disturbed; and do not permit yourselves to be fearful and intimidated and cowardly and unsettled.]"

**Psalm 37:37 (NIV):** "Consider the blameless, observe the upright; a future awaits those who seek peace."

AMPC: "Mark the blameless man and behold the upright, for there is a happy end for the man of peace."

**Job 22:21 (NIV):** "Submit to God and be at peace with him; in this way prosperity will come to you."

AMPC: " Acquaint now yourself with Him [agree with God and show yourself to be conformed to His will] and be at peace; by that [you shall prosper and great] good shall come to you."

## Day three

# Day three

*Day three*

# Day four

## Prayer

Jehovah Shalom, let mercy, peace, and love be multiplied to me. You are the God of my peace, and it is you that will crush Satan under my feet. O Lord, reveal to me to me the abundance of peace and truth. Bring healing and wholeness to my body and my life. Sustain me with your peace and guide me in the way of righteousness. Produce a harvest of righteousness and peace within me. I know that your thoughts towards me are of peace and not evil. Today, help me to mind the things of your Spirit; therefore, life and peace are mine. In Jesus' name. Amen.

## Confession

I receive the peace of God that passes all understanding.
The peace of God will guard my heart and my mind.
Jehovah will keep me in perfect peace.
Because the Lord has set His affection upon me, I will not fear.

# Scriptures for Meditation

**Romans 16:20 (NIV):** "he God of peace will soon crush Satan under your feet. The grace of our Lord Jesus be with you."

AMPC: "And the God of peace will soon crush Satan under your feet. The grace of our Lord Jesus Christ (the Messiah) be with you."

**Jeremiah 33:6 (NIV):** "'Nevertheless, I will bring health and healing to it; I will heal my people and will let them enjoy abundant peace and security.'"

AMPC: "Behold, [in the future restored Jerusalem] I will lay upon it health and healing, and I will cure them and will reveal to them the abundance of peace (prosperity, security, stability) and truth."

**Romans 8:6 (NIV):** "The mind governed by the flesh is death, but the mind governed by the Spirit is life and peace."

AMPC: "Now the mind of the flesh [which is sense and reason without the Holy Spirit] is death [death that [a]comprises all the miseries arising from sin, both here and hereafter]. But the mind of the [Holy] Spirit is life and [soul] peace [both now and forever]."

**Jude 2 (NIV):** "Mercy, peace and love be yours in abundance."

AMPC: "May mercy, [soul] peace, and love be multiplied to you."

**Hebrews 12:11 (NIV):** "No discipline seems pleasant at the time, but painful. Later on, however, it produces a harvest of righteousness and peace for those who have been trained by it."

AMPC: "For the time being no discipline brings joy, but seems grievous and painful; but afterwards it yields a peaceable fruit of righteousness to those who have been trained by it [a harvest of fruit which consists in righteousness—in conformity to God's will in purpose, thought, and action, resulting in right living and right standing with God]."

# Day four

# Day four

# Day four

# Day five

## Prayer

O Lord, let your face shine upon me and give me your peace. I know that you have redeemed my soul in peace from the battle that was against me. Now, Lord, I dwell in a peaceful habitation, in secure dwellings, and in quiet resting places. Thank you for counting my household worthy of your peace. My children will be taught by you, O Lord, and their peace will be great. Father, You are my peace and have made me one with you. I no longer worry concerning tomorrow or what is to come. I have decided to remain in your love and in your peace. Great is your peace upon me. In Jesus' name. Amen.

## Confession

Though I walk through valleys, I will fear no evil, for God is with me. I refuse to be tormented by the devil, vexed, harassed, oppressed, poor or broke. I have been redeemed from the curse of the law.

# Scriptures for Meditation

**Numbers 6:26 (NIV):** "the Lord turn his face toward you and give you peace.'"

AMPC: "The Lord lift up His [approving] countenance upon you and give you peace (tranquility of heart and life continually)."

**Psalm 55:18 (NIV):** "He rescues me unharmed from the battle waged against me, even though many oppose me."

AMPC: "He has redeemed my life in peace from the battle that was against me [so that none came near me], for they were many who strove with me."

**Matthew 10:13 (NIV):** "If the home is deserving, let your peace rest on it; if it is not, let your peace return to you."

AMPC: "Then if indeed that house is deserving, let come upon it your peace [that is, freedom from all the distresses that are experienced as the result of sin]. But if it is not deserving, let your peace return to you."

**Isaiah 32:18 (NIV):** "My people will live in peaceful dwelling places, in secure homes, in undisturbed places of rest."

AMPC: "My people shall dwell in a peaceable habitation, in safe dwellings, and in quiet resting-places."

**Judges 6:24 (NIV):** "So Gideon built an altar to the Lord there and called it The Lord Is Peace. To this day it stands in Ophrah of the Abiezrites."

AMPC: "Then Gideon built an altar there to the Lord and called it, The Lord is Peace. To this day it still stands in Ophrah, which belongs to the Abiezrites.

# Day five

# Day five

# Day five

# Day six

## Prayer

Peace is only found in you, Jesus, my Lord and Savior. Therefore, I am the rightful owner of God's shalom. I use peace as my servant to remain in a place of rest in my Father. This day, Lord, I choose to be steadfast and unmovable, always abounding in the work of the Lord and always walking in peace towards others. Allow, Holy Spirit, to minister through me your peace to my surroundings and all I come in contact with. This day, my peace will pave the way for solutions, calm troubled waters, and cause me to enjoy the life I have in the day I have been given. Father, thank you for the peace of God which is now in complete operation in my life. In Jesus' name. Amen.

## Confession

The Lord is my banner.
The Lord is my refuge.
I bring peace to others.
Peace is my atmosphere.

# Scriptures for Meditation

**Isaiah 53:5 (NIV):** "But he was pierced for our transgressions, he was crushed for our iniquities; the punishment that brought us peace was on him, and by his wounds we are healed."

AMPC: " But He was wounded for our transgressions, He was bruised for our guilt and iniquities; the chastisement [needful to obtain] peace and well-being for us was upon Him, and with the stripes [that wounded] Him we are healed and made whole."

**1 Corinthians 15:58 (NIV):** "Therefore, my dear brothers and sisters, stand firm. Let nothing move you. Always give yourselves fully to the work of the Lord, because you know that your labor in the Lord is not in vain.

AMPC: "Therefore, my beloved brethren, be firm (steadfast), immovable, always abounding in the work of the Lord [always being superior, excelling, doing more than enough in the service of the Lord], knowing and being continually aware that your labor in the Lord is not futile [it is never wasted or to no purpose].

**Hebrews 4:3 (NIV):** Now we who have believed enter that rest, just as God has said, "So I declared on oath in my anger, 'They shall never enter my rest.'" And yet his works have been finished since the creation of the world.

AMPC: "For we who have believed (adhered to and trusted in and relied on God) do enter that rest, in accordance with His declaration that those [who did not believe] should not enter when He said, As I swore in My wrath, They shall not enter My rest; and this He said although [His] works had been completed and prepared [and waiting for all who would believe] from the foundation of the world."

**Romans 12:18 (NIV):** "If it is possible, as far as it depends on you, live at peace with everyone."

TLB: "Don't quarrel with anyone. Be at peace with everyone, just as much as possible."

**Mark 4:39 (NIV):** "He got up, rebuked the wind and said to the waves, "Quiet! Be still!" Then the wind died down and it was completely calm."

AMPC: "And He arose and rebuked the wind and said to the sea, Hush now! Be still (muzzled)! And the wind ceased (sank to rest as if exhausted by its beating) and there was [immediately] a great calm (a perfect peacefulness)."

## Day six

# Day six

## Day six

# Day seven

## Prayer

Lord, I am thankful that Jesus is my Prince of Peace. Therefore, I will walk in your prosperity and peace every day. I refuse to be tormented by the devil, vexed, harassed, oppressed, poor or broke. You, O Lord, have redeemed me from the curse of the law. I refuse to live any longer without the peace of God in my life. Jesus was chastised for my peace. Father, I receive now, my covenant right to walk in Your glorious shalom. I am not waiting on peace to arrive. I possess it right now and in abundance. Thank you, Lord, that I can share my peace freely with others as it has freely been given to me. I will not judge those who are without Your peace but rather win them to You, Lord, with the forerunner of peace. My life is forever changed because of the mercies you have shown and the revelation knowledge of shalom. Thank you, Father, for your great provision of peace. In Jesus' name. Amen.

## Confession

He is my Jehovah Shalom, my prosperity, and my peace.
He only is my rock and my salvation: He is my defense; I shall not be moved.
I will walk in peace all the days of my life.

# Scriptures for Meditation

**Isaiah 9:6 (NIV):** "For to us a child is born, to us a son is given, and the government will be on his shoulders. And he will be called Wonderful Counselor, Mighty God, Everlasting Father, Prince of Peace."

AMPC: "For to us a Child is born, to us a Son is given; and the government shall be upon His shoulder, and His name shall be called Wonderful Counselor, Mighty God, Everlasting Father [of Eternity], Prince of Peace."

**Galatians 3:13 (NIV):** "Christ redeemed us from the curse of the law by becoming a curse for us, for it is written: "Cursed is everyone who is hung on a pole."

AMPC: "Christ purchased our freedom [redeeming us] from the curse (doom) of the Law [and its condemnation] by [Himself] becoming a curse for us, for it is written [in the Scriptures], Cursed is everyone who hangs on a tree (is crucified);

**James 4:7 (NIV):** "Submit yourselves, then, to God. Resist the devil, and he will flee from you."

AMPC: "So be subject to God. Resist the devil [stand firm against him], and he will flee from you."

**Numbers 25:10-13 (NIV):** "The Lord said to Moses, "Phinehas son of Eleazar, the son of Aaron, the priest, has turned my anger away from the Israelites. Since he was as zealous for my honor among them as I am, I did not put an end to them in my zeal. Therefore tell him I am making my covenant of peace with him. He and his descendants will have a covenant of a lasting priesthood, because he was zealous for the honor of his God and made atonement for the Israelites."

AMPC: "And the Lord said to Moses, Phinehas son of Eleazar, the son of Aaron the priest, has turned my wrath away from the Israelites, in that he was jealous with My jealousy among them, so that I did not consume the Israelites in My jealousy. Therefore say, Behold, I give to Phinehas the priest My covenant of peace. And he shall have it, and his descendants after him, the covenant of an everlasting priesthood, because he was jealous for his God and made atonement for the Israelites.

**Romans 8:14 (NIV):** "For those who are led by the Spirit of God are the children of God.

TPT: "The mature children of God are those who are moved by the impulses of the Holy Spirit."

## Day seven

# Day seven

# Day seven

# *Additional Scriptures for Meditation*

"I am The-Lord-Is-Peace [Jehovah Shalom]"
-*Judges 6:24*

"For the Kingdom of God is not eating and drinking,
but righteousness and peace and joy in the Holy Spirit."
-*Romans 14:27*

"He who would love life and see good days, let him refrain his tongue from evil, and his lips from speaking deceit. Let him turn away from evil and do good; let him seek peace and pursue it."
-*1 Peter 3:10-11*

"Blessed (enjoying enviable happiness, spiritually prosperous—with life-joy and satisfaction in God's favor and salvations regardless of their outward conditions) are the makers and maintainers of peace, for they shall be called the sons of God!"
- *Matthew 5:9, AMP*

"If it is possible, as much as depends on you,
live peaceably with all men."
-*Romans 12:18*

"But the fruit of the Spirit is love, joy, peace, forbearance, kindness, goodness, faithfulness, gentleness and self-control.
Against such things there is no law."
-*Galatians 5:22-23*

"Make every effort to live in peace with everyone and to be holy; without holiness no one will see the Lord."
-*Hebrews 12:14*

"But the wisdom that comes from heaven is first of all pure; then peace-loving, considerate, submissive, full of mercy and good fruit, impartial and sincere."
*-James 3:17*

# Final thoughts

*His Peace*

# Prayer of Salvation

Father, I come to you in the name of Jesus. Your word says: "That if thou shalt confess with thy mouth the Lord Jesus, and shalt believe in thine heart that God hath raised him from the dead, thou shalt be saved. I do that now. I confess Jesus Christ as my Lord and Savior, and I believe that you have raised Him from the dead. Thank you for saving me. I am now a child of the Most High God.

In Jesus Name!

Amen!

www.ingramcontent.com/pod-product-compliance
Lightning Source LLC
Chambersburg PA
CBHW071410290426
44108CB00014B/1769